DYING FOR HEAVEN...?

Derek Gravatt

DayOne

© Day One Publications 2019
First printed 2019

ISBN 978-1-84625-651-6

Unless otherwise indicated Scripture quotations in this publication are from the Holy Bible, New International Version (NIV), copyright © 1973, 1978, 1984, International Bible Society. Used by permission of Hodder and Stoughton, a member of the Hodder Headline Group. All rights reserved.

British Library Cataloguing in Publication Data available

Published by Day One Publications
Ryelands Road, Leominster, HR6 8NZ
Telephone 01568 613 740
Toll Free 888 329 6630 (North America)
email—sales@dayone.co.uk
web site—www.dayone.co.uk

Cover design by Kathryn Chedgzoy

Printed by 4edge Limited

DYING FOR HEAVEN...?

Contents

Preface

The foundational material of this book hit the airwaves long before it reached the printed page. The congregation of Otford Evangelical Free Church in Kent were the first recipients of these messages in the Autumn of 2005 when I was their pastor. The original nine-part series of evening sermons was then entitled *The death of the righteous* based on Balaam's enigmatic wish recorded in Numbers 23:

'Let me die the death of the righteous,
and may my end be like theirs.'

Such an extraordinary statement excited my curiosity. It seemed to me to be of immense importance. That was what led me to explore the subject more deeply. Exactly what is 'the death of the righteous?'

My prayer for this book is threefold:

Firstly, that it will open up for Christians the subject of death, which is seldom discussed among us, or, then only with trite phrases and slick answers.

Secondly, that God would be pleased to use it for the strengthening of believers' faith against that 'last enemy'.

Thirdly, that it may help those who do not have saving faith in Jesus Christ to see how and why Christians are able to grieve hope*fully* and not hope*lessly*, and in so doing would themselves come to join the ranks of those who will die 'the death of the righteous.'

And I wrote it, too, because I need these truths as much as anyone else.

Soli Deo gloria

DBG

1 Balaam

Please read Numbers 22 – 24

This passage relates the history of Balaam, an extraordinary and enigmatic figure. He was a professional prophet—that is, he made his living by predicting the future and by proclaiming blessings or curses on peoples and situations. He was obviously very successful, and this is what brought him into the history of God's people, the Israelites. He is frequently confirmed by the Bible text as an unbeliever. That does not mean that he doubted the existence and activity of God; the existence and activity of God was quite accepted by Balaam. He even knew that God was the LORD, which, when written in capitals in our modern translations signifies the covenant-making and covenant-keeping God and is the way by which those who are in covenant relationship with him, people we now call Christians, may and do address him. No; what the Bible means by the designation 'unbeliever' is a person who will not trust in, nor entrust themselves to, the LORD God.

Balaam enters the history of God's people as they are gathered on the plains of Moab, east of the River Jordan, preparing to enter the Promised Land. Neighbouring kings had put up different types of opposition to their advance, so far to no avail. Balak, King of Moab, had seen what had happened to the nations that had opposed the children of Israel by force, and he and his people, the Moabites, were terrified. So he decided on a completely different approach:

he had the idea of putting a curse on the Israelites, thinking that this would solve his territorial problem. As soon as he had had that idea he knew of no-one better to implement it than Balaam. Everyone knew that Balaam was at the top of his game, the best in the business. Of course, such expertise did not come cheaply, but the anticipated gains meant that Balak had no difficulty convincing his treasury officials to amend that year's defence budget.

The Moabite delegation seemed to know Balaam's scale of fees. What they weren't prepared for was his reply! Overnight God had appeared personally to Balaam and told him that the Israelites were not to be cursed because they were blessed (obviously meaning by the LORD God himself). You will see from the subsequent history of bargaining, trading on Balaam's love of money, and with the directing voice of God, that Balaam does indeed end up pronouncing blessing on the people of God. Contrary to Balak's wishes and the Moabites' money, Balaam can only submit to God. And it is during his first prophetic oracle, as he looks down from a mountain on God's people, that he utters these extraordinary and remarkable words, **'Let me die the death of the righteous'** (23:10b).

What is 'the death of the righteous?' Sometimes unbelievers throw up the best questions! Firstly, Balaam must have had an awareness that there was more than one way to die, otherwise there would be no point to what he said. Secondly, it implies that Balaam must have seen the death of a righteous person, and so must have been able to distinguish such a death from that of an *un*righteous person, that is, all those who did not fall into the category of 'righteous', whatever that might be. Thirdly, his statement is in the form of a wish prayer: this means that Balaam must have had an understanding that the death of the righteous, or the way that they died, was something very desirable, and therefore something that he wanted very much for himself. Fourthly, this exclamation must mean that he did not regard himself as one of the righteous (although it is clear that he knew God) for otherwise he would never have added, '**May my end be like theirs.**'

But these observations clearly take us back further to the subject of death itself. Why is this subject so important? There are several reasons. Firstly, because we all have to die; it is the one certainty of our lives (Hebrews 9:27). Secondly, because death is **the last enemy** (1 Corinthians 15:26). Thirdly, it is foolish not to think about it (Deuteronomy 32:29). Fourthly, because it is a taboo subject. Regrettably it is not only a taboo subject in everyday company but also in Christian circles, even among those who vigorously declare that they are Bible-believing Christians. In the last of these it is often disguised by pious-sounding platitudes frequently trotted out, for example 'being with Christ is far better,' usually meaning for other people's Christian relatives or friends, but noticeably not always done with the same eagerness when it's their own. So it is important that we avoid hypocrisy and unreality.

The use of the Bible as our textbook might lead some to complain that many of the deaths recorded in it are violent, the implication being that those are not relevant to most of us. But death is a violence, a violation of God's original order. We need to be powerfully reminded of that truth. Not only that, but God very often teaches us by extremes in order to wake us from our spiritual lethargy so that we recognise and receive his message. He does not want us to miss the point! Finally, we need this teaching about death so that we are equipped to encourage and strengthen our fellow-Christians, and to be able to explain to unbelievers why we do not grieve hope*less*ly when a fellow-Christian dies (1 Thessalonians 4:13–14, 1 Peter 3:15).

But first, even more fundamentally, what is death? Physical death is the transition from this earthly existence to an eternal existence. We are mortal by nature, that is, we are subject to death. And there is a beyond. People can try and deny this but it cannot be avoided because God has built that into us (Ecclesiastes 3:11). And it is exactly this inability to totally deny eternity (or that dimension), as for example the thought that one's dead relatives still exist 'somewhere', that makes it imperative to answer the question of, 'What next?' The Bible tells us why this is an urgent question. There are two reasons: firstly, because after death we face judgement (Ecclesiastes 3:17, 12:14, Hebrews 9:27); and secondly, because none of us knows when we are going to die (Ecclesiastes 9:12).

The ultimate riddle with Balaam is this: knowing what he knew, that there truly was a God, a transcendent and good LORD, and that there was a possibility and a desirability of dying righteous, why did he not take steps to become righteous and achieve the answer to his own prayer? This is, of course, the ultimate riddle of sin, that which we are which makes us intrinsically not right with God. I hope that no reader will stay a Balaam but will come to know for themselves that they will **die the death of the righteous.**

2 Abel

Please read Genesis 4:1–16, Hebrews 11:4, 6

We have already seen that Balaam wanted to die the death of the righteous. What did he see that made such a death desirable? We shall study Bible characters in order to understand what *God* means by **the death of the righteous**. On the face of it many of them do not appear to have had very desirable deaths. They are mostly dramatic headline stuff. And that is exactly the point. It is as if God is writing in capitals; he doesn't want us to miss the point. This tells us that there must be something more than meets the eye. So we shall look at these deaths, each with its particular contribution to understanding the full truth, in order to find that 'something.' The first is that of Abel.

His name means *vapour* or *breath*. We are immediately reminded of the brevity, the transitory nature, of human life. We need to remember that! Abel's is the first death recorded in the Bible. That would be a good enough reason by itself to study it. But it is even more important in a paradigmatic sense in that it was the death of a righteous person. This verdict about Abel is clearly confirmed for us by Jesus himself (see Matthew 23:35). .

What made Abel righteous? It was that both he and his offering were accepted by God. For anyone or anything to be accepted by God they or it must be righteous. Abel's acceptance was nothing to do with the work that he did—

otherwise we would all have to be shepherds! It was nothing to do with the fact that Cain's offering did not include blood sacrifice. We can say this confidently because the word used for their offerings is the same for both men, and it is the word used elsewhere for grain-offerings. This word is never used of a burnt offering where an animal is killed. It has the connotation of a gift, voluntarily given, or tribute, something brought by a lesser person to a greater one.

But more: **The LORD looked with favour on Abel and his offering, but on Cain and his offering he did not look with favour**. There was no separation between either man and his offering. Why? Because an offering shows the state of a person's heart, what is really going on inside. Look at what happened. **Cain brought some of the fruits of the soil**. He had no respect for God. He was not acknowledging God as the greatest, and certainly not as the greatest in his life. Abel gave the best that he could to God, **fat portions from some of the firstborn of his flock**. He was making a statement with his goods that acknowledged God's worth, his right to first claim on Abel's life.

That phrase **look with favour on** is a word entailing forgiveness when the lesser brings a gift like this. So the acceptance of the gift signifies acceptance of the person. After all, God does not need our gifts; a relationship with him is not a relationship of equals. And this is proved by answering the question, 'How?' How did Abel gain God's favour? Answer: **by faith. By faith Abel offered God a better sacrifice than Cain did. By faith he was commended as a righteous man, when God spoke well of his offerings**. Notice the intimate connection between person and offering. Why is that so important? Because: **without faith it is impossible to please God, because anybody who comes to him must believe that he exists and that he rewards those who earnestly seek him.**

And that was not a flash in the pan. This was an ongoing, persevering faith. That is why the Bible says **God spoke well of his offerings.** This is why I do not think that the murder took place immediately after offering number 1. This view is confirmed by 1 John 3:12. There we are told that Abel's **actions were righteous,** that is, not just his offerings. And this verse also tells us why Abel died, the ultimate reason he was murdered: Cain's **actions were evil** because he **belonged to the Evil One.** What or who you worship matters. It governs life and lifestyle. If you are not righteous then you are unrighteous. God makes it clear in the Bible that there are only these two categories, and that they are absolute. Furthermore the unrighteous cannot abide the righteous. That is the living proof of their unrighteousness, the fact that they are not accepted by God.

This being so, however, why is a death such as Abel's to be desired, and to be desired greatly? And not just to be desired greatly, but to be attained? Because it gives the right perspective on life, focusing on our ultimate destination. Our lives are supposed to be God-ward because we are made for him. So the particular lesson of the death of Abel is: if we are right with God, then there is nothing else and no-one else to worry about; no-one can take that relationship from us—ever!

So from Abel's history we learn:

1 Knowing God is insufficient. Cain did.
2 Coming before God is insufficient. Cain did.

3 Coming before God with an offering is insufficient. Cain did.

4 We *must* come before God in the right way, the way that he has stipulated (see John 4:24). To do that we must come **by faith**. And the same is true about our offerings because the offering is inseparable from the person. The offering exposes the truth or otherwise of our worship, whether or not God is truly the greatest in our affections, and hence in our lives.

And if we are not? Note the grace of God to Cain. Did Cain deserve to have God speak to him? Of course not! Yet God came. There was an opportunity to repent and receive acceptance. Cain could never say that God did not care. Neither can you. God's grace is available now.

Why didn't Balaam die righteous? Why didn't Cain? Why don't you? Is it love of this life? (See Matthew 6:24.) Or is it thinking we know better than God—which is not only rebellious but ridiculous? Are you ready to die? You are only ready to die if you are going to die the death of the righteous. And that means that both you and your offering must be acceptable to God. And that is possible only through Jesus Christ. **I urge you, in view of God's mercy, to offer your bodies as living sacrifices, holy and pleasing to God, which is your spiritual act of worship** (Romans 12:1). **And by faith Abel still speaks, even though he is dead.** Abel died the death of the righteous.

3 Naboth

Please read 1 Kings 21

In the previous chapter we saw that dying the death of the righteous means dying as one who is the right with God. But what does that mean *practically* for the Christian in the real world, every day? How does that work out in life *now*? There is a hint in 1 John 3:12 where it refers to the *actions* of Abel as righteous. We know we are not talking about doing good deeds to earn salvation and a sure hope of heaven, because we were able to show that Abel was already accepted by God; his righteous actions came as a *result* of that acceptance. We now want to know what are the actions of someone who has already been commended by God as righteous, or, to use the analogy found in John 8:39, the proof of one's new spiritual parentage. And we need to answer this question because there are some professed Christians who think that once they have got the vertical (God) relationship sorted there's nothing else to worry about or do—they can get on with life just like everybody else. But that is not the Bible's view.

1 Kings 21 confronts us with the reality of everyday. Verse 25 shows us the society in which Naboth lived as showcased by its ruling couple. It was **evil** as defined by what God thinks (**in the eyes of the LORD**). God's righteous standard was the guidance that was missing. It was also a society **going after idols**. Idols are a mirage, unreal, dead and impotent. They provide the right climate for evil to flourish because they

avoid making any absolute judgements. This automatically results in a further evil, that of simply 'letting' things happen. (Note that this event follows the events of chapters 17 and 18, which makes all of it much worse.)

This was the environment in which Naboth, a righteous man, lived. Naboth was sitting on a spiritual time-bomb. And I think he knew it. 1 Kings 21 tells us when it detonated. The world's requests often seem very reasonable. Most of our temptations do not come with a label 'THIS IS A TEMPTATION WHICH COULD SERIOUSLY DAMAGE YOUR SPIRITUAL HEALTH.' Indeed, there is often a positive spiritual pressure, for example **living at peace with all men** (Romans 12:18). The devil is perfectly capable of using Bible truth to his advantage as can be seen in his temptation of Jesus (Matthew 4:6), where he gives half a Scripture out of context, a favourite device. In Naboth's case it was the issue of respect for authority. But the Bible makes it clear that the authority we are to respect above all others is God's; where there is a conflict, his must prevail, as shown very clearly in Acts 5:29.

How did Naboth cope? He brought God into the situation: **'The LORD forbid that I should give you the inheritance of my fathers.'** The proposed transaction would have effected a permanent change of title. Naboth's decision was nothing to do with 500 years of family tradition, but altogether to do with God and his Word. It is Naboth's Acts 5:29 moment. But what word? The LORD had said: **The land must not be sold permanently, because the land is mine and you are but aliens and my tenants** (Leviticus 25:23). The land was God's. His people were his tenants. Land could be temporarily sold to meet a financial need but it always had to revert to its original owner in the year of Jubilee. King Ahab was seeking a permanent sale, which was contradictory to God's will.

Naboth knew God's Word, even the small print of Leviticus! How much do you know? How long have you been a Christian? Don't you want to know what he says? Don't say that you are not clever enough. God has promised his Holy Spirit to help us. Many of the Christians in the first century AD were slaves; they understood. Many of the Christians at the time of the Reformation in England were uneducated folk; they understood. Do you get your answers from the Bible? Or do you say, 'I don't know any relevant part of the Bible,' and make up your own wisdom? Naboth unhesitatingly decided his response because he knew what God had said; it was in his Word.

Naboth understood the Scriptures as *God's* Word, and therefore non-negotiable. He did not make excuses such as it not being a major doctrine, or it does not apply to me, or that he was now living in a different century. Adopting any of those approaches means that we are not accepting God's Word as *God's* Word. God expects his children, Christians, to take it seriously. God's Word is a unity. You might think that Naboth's response was over the top. Surely God couldn't have meant him to take it so exactly, so ignore it. Is that what you do, decide which bits are in and which bits are out? Or does that happen only when life gets difficult? And in any case, who decides which bits are in and which bits are out? As God's Word is a unity, any other approach is actually setting your opinions above God's authority. God's Word is then rendered of no use to you. Or do you allow circumstances to govern whether or not you are obedient to God's Word, instead of God's Word guiding you in your circumstances? Naboth could easily have ignored God's Word when he found out that it was going to cost him his life. He had plenty of opportunity. Circumstances are not to be our guide, the Word of God is. For, if not, God is removed from the equation.

Naboth was obedient to God's Word, what God had said. It was that Word which governed his behaviour. If God had laid down certain things, that was good enough for Naboth; in fact, nothing better. Two implications follow. Firstly, that he was willing to suffer for it. Think of the shame, the disgrace. False accusation is so hard to deal with. There was the bitterness of injustice. Think of the emotional pressure: what did Mrs Naboth and the children think? Secondly, he was willing to be obedient to that Word at all costs. For God and his Word are not separable. Naboth was proving his love for God through obedience to his Word. Or, putting it the other way round: obedience to that Word proved his love for God.

Why did Naboth die? After all, he was a model citizen, just the sort we are always told is so necessary—until, that is, such a person gets in the way, gets in the way of a society that is hostile to the Creator God and his Word, and therefore cannot abide any reminder of God's righteousness. Naboth died simply because he was righteous, which shows us the depth of that hostility. If you are a Christian (like Naboth, in the right with God) then you are to live like Naboth. 1 Kings 21 is a reminder that we, too, live in a society that is hostile to the Creator God, literally selling itself to do evil, with a multitude of idolatries, taking what it wants when it wants, by killing if necessary, and where any who speak the truth are labelled the enemy. And don't be fooled by the nice neighbours; when the chips are down they will be like Naboth's neighbours.

How are we to do this? We must live like Naboth, the righteous, who knew God's Word, believed it to be the unchanging Word of the living God, and who obeyed that Word. Naboth was a type (a living picture) of Christ. His righteous living crystallised those unbelievers' rebellion against God, just as Jesus' did. We, too, are meant to portray Christ to the unbelieving world. The righteous can be faithful to death because they know and trust the whole Word of God: **Blessed are those who are persecuted because of righteousness for theirs is the kingdom of heaven** (Matthew 5:10), and **The Lord will rescue me from every evil attack and will bring me safely to his heavenly kingdom** (2 Timothy 4:18). Naboth died the death of the righteous.

4 Stephen

Please read Acts 6:8 – 8:3

Abel taught us that we must be right with God, what the Bible calls righteous. Naboth showed us what it means to live righteously. Stephen is going to show us a life which proclaims righteousness. Together they are helping us build a composite picture of what it means to die the death of the righteous.

Stephen was the leading light among the first deacons. (The seven are not called deacons in Acts 6 but the principles of what deacons are and do is established here.) His life demonstrates powerfully that every believer is called to, and responsible for, evangelism. Part of evangelism is contending for the truth. Stephen's speech here is the longest in the whole of Acts. Now God never wastes words. Whenever lengthy dialogue occurs in the Bible an important issue is at stake; in this case it is there to advance the author's case for proclaiming and clarifying the truth. That is exactly what God was doing through Stephen: he was dealing with the disobedience and idolatry of the Jews. It is the truth of the gospel of Jesus Christ that it does not belong in the Promised Land or Jerusalem. So Stephen was not meandering aimlessly or boringly through history but being intensely purposeful. Where did God appear to Abraham? Mesopotamia. Where did Joseph succeed? Egypt. Where did Jacob die? Egypt. Where did Moses grow up? Egypt. Where did Moses flee to? Midian. Where did God appear to Moses? Sinai. Where did

God send Moses? Egypt. Did Moses ever enter the Promised Land? No. With that as background, Stephen then moved on to deal with the issues raised by his opponents. Where did Israel receive the law? Mount Sinai. Where did Israel have the tabernacle? In the wilderness. So neither law nor covenant nor tabernacle originated in the Promised Land. What was Israel's response to the law they said they venerated? They refused to obey it, and still did not do so. What did Israel know about the Creator God who had rescued them? They knew very well that he did not live in houses or a temple. What did they do with that knowledge? They ignored it and idolised their temple and their land. And worse: the typical Old Testament reaction to the prophets God sent to his people to point out their sins was to kill them. The most common reaction to God's prophets who prophesied about a Messiah was to kill them. The climax of this history was the killing of Jesus, God's ultimate prophet, who was indeed the Messiah.

What was the weapon Stephen used? God's Word. Alone. He obviously had a thorough knowledge of God's Word. More importantly, he understood that Word and so knew how to use it. And he had the Holy Spirit's help. Stephen himself is an exposition of Philippians 3:10–11. **I want to know Christ**. How? Through **the power of his resurrection and the fellowship of sharing in his sufferings**. Stephen followed exactly the Christ pattern: he told the truth of the Word of God; he was hated without reason; he was opposed by false witnesses; he defended himself but his opponents were not willing to listen; they took him outside their precious city to kill him; while dying he forgave his enemies. But his death achieved both his personal vindication and the complete frustration of his enemies' plans. Stephen had witnessed to Christ; Christ then witnessed to Stephen by standing to welcome him to glory.

What did his death achieve? His death spoke to at least one unbeliever, Saul, who was later converted and became the apostle Paul. It caused others, like the burial party, to stand publicly for Christ. And it resulted in the spread of the gospel. God used his death, violent though it was. We are all keen, I hope, for God to use our lives. But what about our deaths? Are you willing for God to use your death in his purposes? Will you die the death of the righteous? Will you, like Stephen, radiate Christ in your death?

What was Stephen's secret? He knew Jesus not only as the Righteous One, but also as the Son of Man. This rich title for Jesus carries the freight of his incarnation, his saving death and resurrection, his heavenly exaltation, and his universal dominion. Is that your understanding of who Jesus Christ is? Why couldn't Stephen have lived? Because he'd taken up his cross to follow Christ (Luke 14:27): he loved Christ more than his own life. He understood the one of old who said, **'Your love is *better* than life'** (Psalm 63:3), and lived that truth.

Does Stephen's history, therefore, challenge your value systems, your priorities in life? Do you know God's Word, which is the only weapon you are given in serving Jesus? Do you understand it so that you can actually **give a reason for the hope that you have** (1 Peter 3:15)? Does his life and witness challenge your obedience? Stephen's death was not in vain. God is always using the weak things of this world to confound the strong (1 Corinthians 1:27). The Jewish authorities sought to stifle the gospel. Their actions simply

DYING FOR HEAVEN...?

made it more potent, multiplying its proclaimers and spreading them more widely.

Final thoughts. Stephen's history helps us to understand the enigma of Psalm 116:15—**Precious in the sight of the LORD is the death of his saints.** The psalmist had praised God for his deliverance from death (v. 3). Yet here is this amazingly confident assertion. How do we explain this? The answer is in verse 8: **For you, O LORD have delivered my soul from death, my eyes from tears, my feet from stumbling, that I may walk before the LORD in the land of the living.** Once assured of deliverance from spiritual death the psalmist was able to see physical death from the Divine perspective. This is what Stephen believed. The proof of the genuineness of his faith is that Christ personally welcomed him to that ultimate land of the living, to heaven itself. We may not receive the vision, but we can have the same welcome. Stephen died the death of the righteous.

5 Samson

Please read Judges 13 – 16, Hebrews 11:32

What a mass of contradictions! What do most people know about Samson? They have heard of Samson and Delilah. They might know the origin of the phrase 'brought the house down!' But *the righteous*? An example to us?? You cannot be serious! But God has said, 'Yes,' and popped him into the Hebrews 11 Faith Hall of Fame to make sure we get the message. On that point, I find it strange how much Christians want to twist Scripture to justify their understanding of why Jephthah is included alongside Samson, and do so by applying 21st century ethics and their own prejudices to a man who lived over 1000 years before Christ, yet never complain about the inclusion of Samson who was serially unfaithful in his dealings with the opposite sex. All of which confirms how contradictory Christians are. But God is not contradictory. God purposely chose this man, with his many and obvious faults, to demonstrate again the truth of Romans 5:20, that **where sin increased grace increased all the more.** Speaking personally, I'm very encouraged!

But how do we get a handle on what God wants to teach us through Samson? The first clue is Bible space. This is always a good guide. Samson's history takes four chapters of the Bible. God doesn't waste words! He is not trying to entertain us. This is not a film studio primer. Four chapters mean the lesson(s) must be very important. Not only that, but unusually there is a whole chapter devoted to Samson's birth. None of the other judges gets this treatment. Why? Because in that chapter there is revealed something about Samson that is Biblically unique. **He grew and the LORD blessed him,** *and the Spirit of the LORD began to stir him*. Here is the key to understanding this most complex of men.

This leads us to the second clue, the context of Samson's life, namely the gross apathy of the people of God. They were oppressed by the Philistines, who represent the forces hostile to our God. But the Israelites were apparently not upset by that state of affairs. They simply left God out, despite the fact that it was he who had put them in that position. For forty years! The significance of forty years meant that a whole generation had grown up with that as the norm; they knew nothing else. That was Samson's generation and what made him unique in his generation was his sense of the wrongness of that situation, his refusal to accept the *status quo*, and the need to do something about it.

Samson recognised the real enemy, the Philistines. And he never lost sight of the fact that they were ENEMY, big-time. But the majority of his fellow-countrymen failed to see that truth. In fact their lifestyle confirmed them in UN-truth; they were all for the quiet life. This is proved emphatically by the disgraceful episode of 15:9–16. Here were the children of Israel of the tribe of Judah who could not raise up an army to oppose the Philistines but could somehow miraculously conjure up a force of 3000 to capture Samson! How abject is that! For one man! And why? Because Samson was upsetting the Philistines; and if the Philistines were upset they would then take it out on them. Were they, or were they not, the people of *God*?

Do we not see the same today: those with a glorious past reduced to apathy, who when their comfort is disturbed and they are reminded of those glorious possibilities, prefer Philistinian slavery to the glorious freedom of the sons of God? Is this us? Samson was not trapped by any political correctness. He understood who the enemy was. They were HIS enemy. And, in fact, so were all who compromised on their allegiance to the LORD God.

Samson's initial methods were wacky but worldly—brute force and personal revenge. They merely highlighted his weaknesses. The unbelieving world can always do those things better. It will always win when those methods are used. But God taught his servant. **The Spirit of the LORD came upon him in power** (15:14). And he *knew* it was God: '*You* **have given your servant this great victory.**' And what he said next showed that he understood its significance: '**Must I now die of thirst and fall into the hands of the** *uncircumcised*'—his way of describing the enemy.

But God had more to do, because the Almighty will not share his glory. God wanted to use him, and was going to use him; but what God wanted even more was Samson himself. That was what the Spirit of the LORD was working towards in the desperate sadness of 16:20 and in the subsequent mercy of 16:22: **But the hair on his head began to grow again.** Hooray! For in the humiliation and loneliness of the prison house was manifest the grace of God. Samson is now at peace. Despite the further humiliation—not what you and I are thinking, but his understanding that he had given the enemies of God occasion to blaspheme—he nevertheless prays to the LORD God, '**O Sovereign LORD, remember**

me. O God, please strengthen me just once more, and let me with one blow get revenge on the Philistines for my two eyes' (16:28). 'Remember me' means act on my behalf because of who you are, the Sovereign. Not Dagon! Samson is still Samson, but now vengeance is committed to God. And that was not so that he could gloat over his enemies: hence **'Let me die with the Philistines.'** This may be difficult to understand, but I think we have here a combination of confession of his own intrinsic worthlessness and faith that God would answer this prayer of faith, faith that God the LORD would collect the glory, not Samson. And God did hear and did answer. God vindicated his servant. That's how we know for certain that Samson's faith was genuine.

These chapters provide a picture of much of the church of Jesus Christ in the UK in the 21st century. Like Judah, which used to be in the vanguard, used to be fighting for God, they are now indiscernible from their Philistine neighbours. They do what the Philistines want. They are upset if their comfort is disturbed. They are also upset if they are reminded that they ought to be different. Their energies are not directed to fighting the enemy but to reinforcing their comforts. There are also many Christians like Mr and Mrs Manoah. They know the rules; they are very reverent toward God; they do a lot of spiritual tut-tutting but they are not involved in this battle. They are bewildered, stuck in a spiritual time-warp. Rules-based Christianity on its own will not take the fight to the enemy.

For all his faults, Samson knew that there was an enemy, and he knew exactly who the enemy was: the unbelieving, idol-worshipping Philistines. He was convinced that they had no place in the Promised Land, and that, therefore, he should be fighting against them, not submitting to them. He had to learn that the weapons of this world are of no use, but that he could depend absolutely on the Spirit of God. His final prayer was a prayer for God to act regardless of what happened to him himself. He was praying to receive God's mercy in spite of his sin and sinfulness. He was a living example of what Jesus said: **'If anyone comes to me and does not hate his father and mother, his wife and children, his brothers and sisters—yes, EVEN HIS OWN LIFE—he cannot be my disciple'** (Luke 14:6). He was one of those whose **weakness was turned to strength** (Hebrews 11:34). Samson died the death of the righteous.

6 Josiah

Please read 2 Chronicles 34 – 35

The first thing we need to understand about Josiah is that he was definitely God's man, which in today's parlance means he was a Christian. Chapter 34 makes that absolutely clear. He is only the second monarch of Judah to be said to **walk in the ways of his ancestor David**, who was the benchmark for fidelity to the LORD God, a fact that is underlined by the phrase **not turning aside to the right or to the left**. And we actually have the record of the progress of his spiritual life: at the age of sixteen he began to seek God, at twenty-six he finds the Book of the Law and is fully converted, with a resultant tremendous passion to worship and serve the living God. All of which leads to an amazing Passover celebration and to setting the temple worship in order again.

Is this revival? Even as all this is going on the prophet Jeremiah understands that, although the King was truly God's man, the nation's heart had not been changed. Then we come to the riddle of 35:20–24. What is your first reaction? How could that be? What a waste! Aged 39! Why? After all, as we're reminded in verse 26, he was definitely a true believer in God. Let's explore.

We need some history before the theology, finding out what God wants to say to us. In Josiah's world the new political reality was the rapid rise in power of Babylon. Assyria, as the world's superpower, was on the way out. And in that transitional phase, when things were in a state of flux, an old-world power, Egypt, sensed an opportunity to flex its military muscles. Egypt was desperate to regain some influence, power and prestige. So Egypt allied herself with a weakened Assyria to try to resist the Babylonian advance. Of course the little players, the small nation states, were desperate to see which way the political wind was blowing. The prophet Isaiah had advised the people of God to trust in God alone. Now, a century later, came the test of that trust. The Egyptians took the initiative and moved northwards in force, intending to join up with the Assyrians in the area of the upper Euphrates to fight against the Babylonians. All of which was too much for Josiah. He mustered his troops and went out to attack the advancing Egyptian army on its route northwards. Why? It wasn't because he was particularly pro-Babylonian. No, it was the sight of Egypt, the original enemy of God's people, trying to tie up with Assyria, the latest enemy of God's people. Any Egyptian project was anathema to Josiah, this one especially so. In Josiah's mind Egypt epitomised all that was anti-God. After all, the children of Israel had been freed by God from Egypt's dominion. The idea of their resurgence via an Assyrian alliance leading to renewed subjugation of Judah would be a contradiction of all that God had savingly accomplished in the past. So in going out to attack Egypt Josiah was standing up for God, and so standing against the forces of evil.

His troops met Neco's on the plains of Megiddo. Egypt's superior forces triumphed; Josiah was killed. However, this battle delayed the Egyptians, who missed their rendezvous with Assyria. By the time they got there the Babylonians had already defeated the Assyrians.

That's the politics and the history. What about the theology, the 'Where was God in all that?' question? It seems at first glance that he is on the Egyptians' side. Neco had told Josiah what God's Word was, not to oppose him. But he had. So Josiah sinned—verse 22. Well, no, actually. Let's re-examine. In that verse it is certainly clear that God is speaking through Neco. Yet compare that with what we read in verse 26 about Josiah's **acts of devotion according to what is written in the Law of the LORD**. And in 2 Kings 22:2 we read **He did what was right in the eyes of the LORD and walked in *all* the ways of his father David**. David was the one who fought God's enemies. We need to apply the Bible as a whole. Egypt was pursuing *her own* ambition, thinking she could trade on the Word of God and use it for her own advantage as opposed to using it for God's glory. God often allows the forces of evil to overreach themselves, thus preparing them for their downfall. So, here is this Word of the LORD in the mouth of an unbeliever. God does that to show that he is in control of *all* things. And if that is so, he can use unbelievers for his purposes and glory, for example Judas and Pilate. He does this, among other reasons, to keep believers humble and stop them taking him for granted.

But here is the Word of the LORD in the mouth of an unbeliever coming true. Yes! And the Word of the LORD in the mouth of an unbeliever known to be so by the believer and the believer not changing tack, fulfilling that Word to their own detriment. What are we to make of that? But this is not the only place in the Bible where this happens. Let me take you to perhaps the key interpretative parallel, John 11:49–53. Caiaphas, the High Priest, is not one of God's men. So the parallel is exact. Did Jesus change tack? No! Why not? Firstly because, as with the Egyptians, Caiaphas is trying to use Divine truth to accomplish his own ends. And secondly, because Jesus already had a Word of God which covered everything, namely, **'I am come to do the will of him who sent me, and his will is that I should lose none of all that he has given me'** (John 6:38–39). The Caiaphas prophecy did not abolish that; it tested it. Jesus' adherence to the prior Word prevailed. Caiaphas' prophecy, undoubtedly true, was within the context of that original Word from God. The same is true, for example, of Abraham being required to sacrifice Isaac, the outcome being explained for us in Hebrews 11:17. Then there is the apostle Paul confronted with the Holy Spirit's word through Agabus; compare Acts 20:23 with 21:11–14. And there are other examples.

These histories confirm that following Christ is following Christ. It is the way of the cross. It is being faithful to death, because we are not our own, we have been bought with a price. We aim to honour God with our bodies. The corollary is, as Abraham showed, to have faith that God will work things out. We look at Josiah at the age of 39 and say, 'What a waste!' as we do about countless Christian martyrs throughout history. But we don't say that about Jesus, do we? Why not?

And *because* we don't say it about Jesus, we must use Jesus Christ and his death on the cross as the lens through which to see Abraham and Paul and Josiah and those countless others, **of whom the world was not worthy, who for the joy set before** them **endured** (Hebrews 11:38, 12:2). The unbelieving world will say to you, 'The Bible says following Jesus will cost you your life.' That is true; Jesus said so (Mark 8:34–35). So would you then stop following Jesus?

What value do you put on your life? It is such a great temptation to value life itself as the world does. How about Paul's evaluation at Acts 20:24? Whose life is it anyway? If you, as a Christian, believe God's Word is true, then you must believe that you have been bought with a price, the greatest price that could ever be paid. That being so, cannot our Lord, the one who is absolutely good, do with your life what pleases him? And do so with your delighted acceptance? Following Jesus means following Jesus. Waste? Look what we are told about God's values: **Precious *in the sight of the LORD* is the death of his saints** (Psalm 116:15). Whose value system are you operating by? Josiah died the death of the righteous.

7 Jonathan

Please read 1 Samuel 31 – 2 Samuel 1

Jonathan highlights, perhaps as no other Bible character except Jesus Christ, the injustice of death, specifically the injustice of *dis*-grace. Some of the men we have looked at had no choice about their deaths. Others had a particular weakness which was a contributory factor. But Jonathan? His death raises questions not hinted at in those other cases.

How much do you know about Jonathan? He was the eldest son of the first king of Israel, Saul. (You need to understand that Saul was definitely *not* one of God's men; 1 Samuel 15 gives the climactic detail of God's dealings with Saul.) Jonathan grew up, therefore, with the expectation that he would be the next king. And that was not because he was bigheaded—because he wasn't, nor because he was greedy— because he wasn't, but simply because he was what we'd call today the 'crown prince.' And he fitted the part in every way. He was indeed a king-in-waiting: he was a man's man, a soldier, courageous, daring, but with great insight and a rare humility; he was loyal and he inspired loyalty.

He found in David a kindred spirit. He was one who discerned early on that David was actually the LORD's anointed in succession to Saul, his father. Jonathan did not whinge spiritually. Rather, he fully embraced the future God had planned, swearing loyalty to David. And he not only swore loyalty but acted loyally, defending David against

Saul's slanderous accusations and assassination attempts. In addition, he encouraged David spiritually at a time when David was greatly discouraged. He did that at great personal cost, and when it would have been so easy to do nothing. Not only did he possess all the necessary qualities to be a superb crown prince, he was truly one of God's men. Yet despite the amount of space he is accorded in the Old Testament he is one of its unsung heroes. Wrongly so! You can read about his life at your leisure, but we are focusing on his death, the death of a righteous one, for we have established that Jonathan is indeed one of the righteous, in the right with God.

The historical context was this: His father King Saul was engaged in fighting the Philistines. At that time they were the most persistent and determined of the enemies of Israel. And they were on the up. So much so that Saul was scared out of his wits. He saw the Philistine forces massed in opposition and **terror filled his heart** (1 Samuel 28:5). It was at that precise moment that Saul confirmed his *un*-Godliness by consulting a medium. In the subsequent battle the Philistines won hands down. That was a great disgrace for Israel, utter ignominy for Saul. Critically wounded, he committed suicide rather than be abused, an example his armour-bearer followed. Jonathan by that time was already dead, being the first of the royal family to be killed in the battle. As you can imagine, the Philistines attributed their victory to their idol-gods. So God's name was disgraced and blasphemed.

2 Samuel 1 highlights the issues:

1   The failure of God's anointed and his people.
2   The fact that Saul and Jonathan are identified together in the same breath is not simply a description of two men

dying from one of the common causes of death to which all humanity is equally exposed. The critical point here is that a believer and an unbeliever died together in a spiritual conflict that failed.

3 Jonathan appeared to share in the disgrace, a disgrace that was not his fault (1:20).

4 Yet Jonathan was unashamed in battle (1:22).

So what are we to learn about the death of the righteous which will give us, ourselves, hope? We begin by asking: how did Jonathan feel? Jonathan knew the truth. He knew that his father was wrong. God was not with Saul. So why go with him? He knew that David was the king-in-waiting. Why not join David? What a temptation! He knew that the battle was lost because the LORD was not with them. No-one likes to be joined to a lost cause, especially if you know that there is a way out.

Jonathan's death is a living exposition of Revelation 2:10–11—**Be faithful, even to the point of death, and I will give you the crown of life**. He was faithful to death in the place God had appointed him—unswervingly so. And because of that, Jonathan shares that eternal promise of Jesus: **He who overcomes will not be hurt at all by the second death**. Was it tragic when Jonathan laid aside a kingdom he could not have in order to enter a Kingdom he could not lose? Jonathan understood that it was the things which are not seen that are eternal (2 Corinthians 4:18). Is that your perspective? Jonathan could have sought his own vindication in this life. It was, and is, a very powerful temptation. It comes to us, too. But if we accept present vindication we shall miss out on the heavenly vindication promised to us by Jesus (Matthew 5:11–12, 6:1). Think about it!

David's gratitude highlights Jonathan's faithfulness to his calling, even when that calling was unrewarded and, in the world's eyes, hopeless. Jonathan had a different role in the Kingdom of God, and he lived it without envy. When failure like this happens it should drive us to prayer. Grief and disgrace are powerfully motivational. David is sure that Philistine pop culture will lampoon Israel's God, his God, and prays against it. Jonathan had died in apparent *dis*-grace. The truth was that he had been fighting for his God, just as he had always done (as, for example, in 1 Samuel 14). He was faithful to death, the death of the righteous. Will you be?

All of which points up the fact that in his death Jonathan was a type of Christ (as indeed every Christian should be). He radiated Christ. His death expounds for us part of the sufferings of Christ as foretold in Isaiah 53. **He was oppressed and afflicted, yet he opened not his mouth**. Jonathan was not a spiritual whinger. **By oppression and judgement he was taken away**. There was an inescapable injustice in his death. **Because he poured out his life unto death**. This was not a passive experience. He died giving his all. There was disgrace for him as well as injustice. But in his death he was faithful to God. **Yet it was the LORD's will to crush him and to cause him to suffer — and the will of the LORD will prosper in his hand**. Jonathan positively accepted his calling. He did not try to evade it. Nor did he dishonour it. But in the will of God it cost him his life.

Precious in the sight of the LORD is the death of his saints. Whether or not he knew the psalm, he knew and experienced its truth. Jonathan died the death of the righteous. Will you?

8 Enoch

Please read Genesis 5:21–24, Hebrews 11:5–6,
and Jude 14–15

W hy is Enoch in this series, for the Bible is explicit that Enoch did *not* experience physical death? Three answers: Firstly, there will be those at the end of time, when Jesus appears, who will not experience physical death, but they will experience *change* (1 Corinthians 15:51). We need to understand this. Enoch's history points this up, a matter which is reinforced by what is said about him in Jude 14–15 when talking about the second coming of the Lord Jesus Christ. Secondly, by having physical death removed from the discussion we are enabled to see the essentials of the transition from NOW to THEN as far as it concerns the righteous. Then, thirdly, this should focus our minds on those essentials both for the NOW and for the WHEN, when Jesus comes again in glory. We'll start at the beginning, in Genesis.

After he became the father of Methuselah, Enoch walked with God three hundred years and had other sons and daughters. The birth of Methuselah is what we call a 'life event'. It was after this that we are told that Enoch **walked with God.** Walking is a Bible metaphor for this life. It implies a journey with a start and a finish, one with an intentional destination. To walk *with* someone there must be an agreed destination, which obviously has to be the same for both parties. The walkers must keep together, otherwise it would

38

hardly be possible to say they were walking *with* each other. As God was the greater in this pairing, and the wording is that Enoch walked with God not that God walked with Enoch, the conclusion must be that Enoch went walking in the God-ward direction. And we can see clearly that this walking with God was something intentional (something Enoch had made up his mind about and wanted to do) and that it started during this earthly life. To walk together for a long period, in this case 300 years, implies companionship.

Enoch walked with God. Notice the repetition of that fact in verse 24. This is God's way in the Bible of underlining something important, something we should especially take note of. **And then he was no more**, that is, no more on this earth. Obviously there was a 'more' **because God took him** (that is, as a person) **away**. Let's be quite clear: this is *not* describing annihilation, nor is it describing a possible reincarnation. It is also equally clear that God's heaven (which is described later for us in the Bible as **a new heavens and a new earth**), is *not* this earth, nor *on* this earth. So we conclude that God must have wanted Enoch to continue to be with him. He took Enoch from this earthly life to himself, to be with him, because he wanted Enoch to go on being with him. And because God is eternal, that meant he would be with him forever.

Hebrews 11 explains all this for us. Enoch was taken from this life, from this sphere of existence, and because of that he did not experience physical death. I am sure that his family looked for him, otherwise it would not say **he could not be found**. Why? Because **God had taken him away**, and what God did was successfully accomplished. In Hebrews we are given the reason for this extraordinary event: **For before he was taken,** he was commended as one who pleased God. Note *before he was taken*; this means that his commendation took place during his this-earthly life. And **commended as one who pleased God**, with the implication that this commendation was by God himself, for who else would know who pleased God? So Enoch shows us that it is possible to be pleasing to God in the life we live now on this earth. How did he do this? The answer is 'by faith'. The precise nature of this faith is spelled out for us here (actually in the negative): **Without faith it is impossible to please God, because anyone who comes to him must believe that he exists and that he rewards those who earnestly seek him**. Enoch clearly had this saving faith, otherwise he could never have walked with God.

That last phrase about reward indicates that there is a division after physical death, the clear implication being that some get this reward and some do not; otherwise the phrase would make no sense. The detail of this is worked out for us in the Jude passage. As early in the history of mankind as the time when Enoch lived there was this understanding that the LORD (that is, God) would come in some final sense, and when he did it would be for the judgement of all mankind. This judgement would result in the conviction of all the ungodly. How did Enoch know this? God must have spoken to him (perhaps when Enoch was walking with God); after all, he was a prophet; and that is exactly what God uses prophets for: **Surely the Sovereign LORD does nothing without revealing his plan to his servants the prophets** (Amos 3:7).

Enoch proclaimed this truth. He also practised it, that is, he lived his life in the light of that truth. Such a life pleased God because it showed that Enoch genuinely believed that God had the power to do what he said would. That is faith. And Biblical faith obeys God. From this we can see the essentials of the death of the righteous. Enoch's example crystallises the issue of seeking God into a belief in his existence and a belief that he has the power to reward those who earnestly seek him; and therefore also that those that are not so rewarded, the ungodly, would be punished. His history also shows that a person must receive God's commendation *before* they die physically. That, after all, was the ground of his being taken away by God from this material existence, to await existence in the new heavens and earth. This shows us that God is more powerful than death. Death was denied because God took him. That, surely, is the very good news of Enoch's history!

It also explains what will happen at the end of time. For at the end of time there will be those who are alive on this earth when the Lord Jesus returns in power and great glory. Enoch's history gives us a foretaste of what will happen to Christians who are alive at that time, those who are commended as pleasing to God because they have trusted savingly in Jesus Christ and have, therefore, had God's adverse judgement against them dealt with through Christ's death on the cross. They will be taken away by God to be with Christ for ever. (These things are explained more fully in 1 Corinthians 15 and 1 Thessalonians 4:13 – 5:11.)

We shall not all sleep (in this context sleep is Bible-speak for death), **but we will all be changed** (1 Corinthians 15:51). Enoch's history shows us exactly what that will be like at the end of time for true Christians, those who are walking with God now in this earthly life.

9 Hezekiah

Please read 2 Kings 18:1–7, 20:1–21,
2 Chronicles 32:24–33 and Isaiah 38 – 39

2 Kings makes it plain by its opening formula common to all the kings that Hezekiah is one of the righteous. He trusted God. He was godly, faithful, blessed by God, and actively promoted the true worship of God. As such, politically he took an anti-Assyrian stance.

But Hezekiah was taken seriously ill **and was at the point of death. 'In the prime of my life,'** as he says; he was suddenly confronted with his own mortality! Contrary to the so-called health and prosperity gospellers, it needs to be said that Christians, like anyone else, will be ill, often seriously so. What Christians need more than anything else when they are seriously ill is to hear God's voice through his Word. That is his grace to them, always. Yes, of course, they need a doctor; but they must not forget their need of God and his Word, especially when confronted with their own mortality. And that is exactly what Hezekiah received through the prophet Isaiah. **'Put your house in order, because you are going to die; you will not recover.'** I wonder if Hezekiah thought of that message as God's *grace* to him!

But it was! For a start, it made Hezekiah pray. Prayer to God is always the right thing to do. His tears confirm the earnestness of this particular prayer. His faith was not great here, but he had sufficient faith to turn to God. We need to remember that Biblically faith is defined primarily by its object, that is who that faith is in, not by any feeling about its subjective strength. Many folk are critical of the apparent selfishness and self-righteousness of Hezekiah's prayer. We need to be careful here because God obviously did not feel that way about it; he heard Hezekiah's prayer and he answered it. The right response for us 21st Century Christians is not to criticise Hezekiah, who lived 700 years before Christ's death and resurrection, but to ask how many of us could truthfully pray such a prayer? When we have sorted out our answer to that question we shall be in the right position for God to teach us from the life of Hezekiah.

Hezekiah tells us what he learned from his near-death experience. Firstly, he was **troubled**. The good thing about his trouble was that it made him go straight to God: **'O LORD, come to my aid!'** He acknowledged that no-one but God could help him. In those days the expectation was that the righteous would live a long life; that would be the proof that they were truly blessed by God. That is why Jesus' disciples asked him, **'Who then can be saved?'** when discussing the position of the rich young ruler (Matthew 19:25). That was exactly why Hezekiah thought he was being **robbed of the rest of my years**. He had to learn that God was sovereign over his life. How about you? It is very easy for Christians to declare with the Psalmist, **'My times are in your hands,'** but how many of us really mean it?!

Secondly, Hezekiah had a renewed consciousness of his sins. This led him to a renewed consciousness of the greatness of God's forgiveness of his sins: **'You have put all my sins behind your back.'** Here is the acknowledgement that forgiveness is something that God has to do, he and no other. It is of his grace, totally undeserved. Wonderfully, this forgiveness from God is a complete forgiveness. I'm guessing—but I think I'm right, because reading it makes me feel the same—that Hezekiah emphasised that word **'all'**. And that is why, despite the fact that this was a very troubling experience, he could say, **'Surely it was for my benefit that I suffered such anguish.'** Being confronted with our own personal mortality crystallises our thinking like nothing else; it concentrates the mind wonderfully! To face death with spiritual equanimity even the righteous need assurance that ALL their sins are forgiven.

God answered his prayer by giving Hezekiah three things: healing, a miraculous sign to confirm his blessing, and another fifteen years of life. Why fifteen years? If you do your sums you will find that this event took place at the midpoint of his reign. So God is giving him a Round 2 of being king. Will Hezekiah be different? To put it another way: will having had the near-death experience, an event which he has acknowledged was for his benefit, change the way he lives?

The event that now matters is recorded in Isaiah 39. Envoys from Babylon came after his illness and recovery. Hezekiah was flattered to think that his fame had spread that far. His response to them was over the top, unwise, and wrong. Did you notice the emphasis in his speech? **'They came to ME. They saw everything in MY palace. There is nothing among MY treasures that I did not show them.'** God's goodness had made him complacent. More, he failed to acknowledge God's goodness, and gave himself glory that rightly belonged to God alone. These circumstances were another test, except that, unlike the near-death experience, it was not obvious to Hezekiah that they were a test. **God left him to test him and to know everything that was in his heart** (2 Chronicles 32:31). How short-lived were the vows made in his 'psalm' (Isaiah 38:10–20)! The Chronicler calls it pride (2 Chronicles 32:25), and so must we.

Facing death was, and is, a critical test for anybody. But facing life is also a critical test. It's just that we don't often see it that way; it's not obvious. That extra fifteen years ended up as a greater test for Hezekiah than the prospect of premature death. The lesson is that we need to live each day as if it were our last. We need to retain the highlighting effect that the imminence of death has upon our consciences. In short, to please God (that is, to live righteously) we need to fear sin *more* than we fear death.

God did something with Hezekiah that, in his mercy, he does not do for us. He gave him extra time, guaranteed. So now put yourself in Hezekiah's shoes. How was it in on the countdown? Fourteen more years ... thirteen, twelve ... still lots of time! Hezekiah fell into the trap of this test of his faith, a test which was actually greater than the test that he had thought was the greatest. What about when there were only three years to go, then two, then one? Now he knew he was going to die; this time there would be no reprieve. It is of God's mercy that we do not know how long we have to live. Then we shall keep that first test in our minds, and keep short accounts with God about our sin. However many years we have been granted, the principle is the same: there is something the Christian should be more afraid of than death, and that is sin.

Did Hezekiah repent? He repented of his Round 1 pride; his 'psalm' shows that. But Isaiah 39 shows that he had to go on learning the lesson. This reminds us not to go on worrying so much about Hezekiah but to challenge ourselves with this question: are our times in God's hands, consciously, gladly so? Then we can concentrate on living for him in the here and now.

Hezekiah, too, died the death of the righteous.

10 Paul

Please read 2 Timothy 3:10 – 4:18

It is one thing to believe that when you die physically you will be with Christ, ready for the new creation, but quite another thing altogether to be spiritually ready to depart this life. Are you ready? This is why we need to look at Paul, who is definitely one of the righteous and is obviously ready to go.

2 Timothy is Paul's last extant epistle, written from a prison in Rome to his spiritual son and loyal lieutenant, Timothy, passing the gospel baton to the next generation. There are many aspects of this letter that make it seem rather like a last will and testament. Because of that it is very personal, and powerful emotions surface. The critical section for our study is 4:6–8. These verses belong in the wider context indicated, which sets the scene for them.

Here is a man who knows that his death is near: **the time has come for my departure.** Such knowledge is not given to every believer. Nevertheless, the way that he describes death is important. The word used here is one used of a ship letting go its moorings at the start of a voyage. In that maritime context that word conveys the following ideas: (a) that, as for any sea voyage, preparation is needed; (b) that of being easily freed from any attachment to the shore, understanding that that is not a difficult task; and (c) suggesting that, although the voyage is expected, its precise departure time is not known, and therefore that there will need to be a perpetual readiness to sail.

What a helpful picture that is! So, applying those ideas to our own deaths: (a) the journey is one that is expected; (b) it is a journey that should be prepared for; (c) that preparation should always be kept in readiness because the departure time is not known; and (d) that it should not be difficult to embark on that journey because the attachments to the current berth are not strong or difficult to break.

Are those things true of you? What are your attachments to this earthly life? Home, family, work, interests, church? All these may be good things. But can you just slip your moorings? Do you even give the matter any thought? Are you ready? Now? And have you prepared? More than that, are you ready for it to happen at any time? Notice there is a difference between preparation and readiness. So the question is: what enabled Paul not to hold on to the things of this world, and even of life itself?

1. His whole life had been a living preparation. He hadn't left it until the last minute. **I am already being poured out like a drink offering.** What does this tell us about his life?

(a) *Being* poured out obviously means that someone else must be doing the pouring out. In his case the implication is that that person is God. He is in God's sovereign hand. And he is content with that. That, after all, is the ultimate preparation.

(b) When Paul uses the imagery of the **drink offering** here he is not thinking in terms of Hebrew worship and Levitical protocols. The choice of imagery relates to the fact that the drink offering was the offering that sailors in those days made to their gods when they slipped their moorings and set out on a voyage. But notice that it is he, himself, who is the offering:

I am already being poured out. So, using the imagery given, who is this offering made to? Like the sailors it will be to his God. Except that Paul's God is not an idol but is the one and only God, the true God, the Creator of all things. To ensure his own safe passage on this journey which he has not taken before (the journey from our time-existence to eternity), he offers up his life to God. Like a drink-offering indicates both the voluntary nature of the offering he was making and that it was meant to be pleasing to his God, the God and Father of our Lord Jesus Christ.

(c) Already shows us that he has been in a state of readiness for a long time.

2. The fact that he was in a state of readiness indicates that he had done his preparation. Do we have any clue what that involved? He tells us, but it is not quite the answer we would have been expecting. I have fought the good fight, I have finished the race, I have kept the faith. These are all descriptions of his life. Firstly, it is likened to a contest. Notice he was not saying, 'I have fought *a* good fight,' which would be referring to the way he had conducted himself, but to the *nature* of the contest he had been engaged in. Secondly, the race: in those days this was over a prescribed course which had to be completed; each Christian life is just like that, and Paul knew that he had reached the end of the course set out for him. Thirdly, and most importantly, he had kept the faith, he had not departed from the truth of the gospel. Immediately we can see that the preparation for dying the death of the righteous is a whole life thing. It is not something done once in the past, like making a will, and then just dusting it down when necessary; rather it is a continuous and continuing

process. Certainly there must be an initial conscious appraisal of the issues. But the way to stay always in readiness is for the whole of one's lived life to be preparation. And it was precisely that which enabled Paul to have a clear conscience.

3. It will be obvious that to be that sort of person, to live life in that sort of way, requires great motivation. Verse 8 tells us what that motivation was: he was certain of his ultimate destiny. His faith was not vague. It was centred on the person of the Lord Jesus Christ, **the Righteous Judge**. Here is where we come full circle. We have been exploring the death of the righteous, and we have come to see that 'righteous' means that a person is right with God, and in the right with God, and that this relationship with God has come about only through God's initiative; it was not something anyone obtained by their own efforts or because of any innate goodness. It is entirely spiritually-logical then that the person through whom this all came about should be the one welcoming such individuals into his presence, **the Lord, the Righteous Judge**. He himself is the standard; therefore he knows exactly who are 'the righteous'.

We also learn one other defining characteristic of the righteous. They are those who **long for his** (that is, Christ's) **appearing**. Because they are folk who hunger and thirst after righteousness they long for that **new heaven and new earth, the home of *righteousness***. This longing is one of the keys to being ready to embark on that final journey without anything or anyone holding us back. When the longing for Christ is strong, it overcomes all other longings, all other attachments. How is it with you? Are you, like Paul, *ready* to die the death of the righteous?

11 Jesus

Please read Isaiah 52:13 – 53:12

This passage is the last of the so-called 'servant songs' in Isaiah (the others are found in chapters 42, 49 and 50). It is the longest and it is climactic. These servant songs are prophecies about the Lord Jesus Christ. It will be remembered that on several occasions Jesus referred to himself as a servant, as for example in Matthew 20:28. Here is the death of the righteous like no other. Let's explore!

The person called the servant in this passage is described as righteous; indeed, at v.11 the wording in the original is emphatic: **the righteous one, my servant.** And this must be so for the passage to make sense. The servant in this prophecy obviously died: **He was assigned *a grave* with the wicked, and with the rich in *his death.*** Yet a verse later we are told **though the LORD makes his life a guilt offering** (these offerings always involved the death of the sacrifice) **he will see his offspring and prolong his days.** The fact that this person truly died and yet did not stay dead but came back to life again is an extraordinary thing. It means that death could not hold on to him. This is proof of this servant's righteousness. It is the exact proof that Peter used when preaching about Jesus on the Day of Pentecost: **'But God raised him from the dead, because it was impossible for death to keep its hold on him'** (Acts 2:24). Impossible? Yes, because death has no hold on those who are 100% righteous; death only has a hold on the unrighteous, people the Bible also refers to as sinners. So, if the righteous servant of Isaiah 53 truly died and then truly came back to life again, the question is, why? What does it mean? What did this death accomplish in the purposes of God?

Even a casual reading of this passage shows that this death was not accidental: **it was the LORD's *will* to crush him, though the LORD *makes* his life a guilt offering,** and **the will of the LORD will prosper in his hand**. And that purpose is shown most clearly when the song says: **My righteous servant will justify many**. The **My** clearly shows that the servant belongs to the LORD God. To justify is a shorthand way of saying to make righteous. By the activity of the servant **many** were going to be made righteous who were currently unrighteous. They could not do that by themselves or for themselves, which is why it required the activity of the Servant.

How? **He will bear their iniquities; he bore the sin of many**. But again, how? For the unbelieving, unrighteous person doesn't know any better, doesn't want to be righteous; that is actually part of the unrighteousness of unrighteousness! That being so, how did the servant come to be the bearer of their iniquities? Answer: **the LORD laid on him the iniquity of us all**; he did that when he made **his life a guilt offering**. Here Isaiah assumes that we know our Leviticus! Chapters 1 to 3 are about worship obligations. Leviticus 4:1 – 6:7 deal with the sin which separates the worshipper from God and makes it impossible for him to offer worship acceptable to God. The first part (4:1 – 5:13) describes the sin offering, the sacrifice necessary to purify the worshipper from the pollution and defilement of sin, and which then makes it possible for him to be forgiven by God. The second part (5:14 – 6:7) describes the guilt offering. This deals with the debt caused by sin; it is about reparation so that the worshipper becomes accepted by God. They are pictures of the effects of Christ's death on the cross. Both are necessary for us to be justified, to be made righteous, 100% acceptable to God (that is as God is righteous). We need to understand God's righteousness if we are to understand the greatness of the salvation that is on offer through Jesus Christ. This salvation is not simply about dealing with our sins; it is far bigger than that. We have fallen short of the glory of God. We have not fulfilled our creation mandate. A debt has been incurred against that glory and it must be settled for us to become acceptable to God. We find both these matters dealt with in Isaiah 53.

There is **the sin offering**. This is to remove the pollution caused by sin, to make atonement, so that we can be forgiven, It tells us that sin is sin, whether it is through ignorance, inadvertence, or intention, and it must be atoned for. In those days the penitent laid his hand on the head of the sacrificial animal, to symbolise the transference of guilt. The animal would then die instead of the sinner who deserved to die. It was killed and its blood sprinkled on the altar. The fat parts were burned as a fragrant offering; the remainder was taken outside the camp and burnt. Can you see how Jesus fulfilled this requirement? When we truly trust in his death it is like that sinner of old putting their hand on the sacrificial victim. Except in our case the transaction is not representative but real: **He was pierced for our transgressions, he was crushed for our iniquities; the punishment that brought us peace was upon him, and by his wounds we are healed. The LORD has laid on him the iniquity of us all.**

But Jesus was also our guilt offering. **My righteous servant will justify many** *and he will bear their iniquities*. And again: **Because he poured out his life unto death ... for he** *bore the sin* **of many**. This transaction means that there is nothing for the trusting sinner to pay. God only requires payment for a debt once; if we accept that Jesus in his death has paid what we owe, then we ourselves have nothing to pay. That means that we are then accepted as righteous!

Christ's death as sin offering means that we can be forgiven by God. Christ's death as a guilt offering means that we can be accepted by God. In summary this is how we can be made righteous, right with God and right for God. And this is not just a mechanical formula. **It was the LORD's will.** God wanted, desired, purposed it. **The Lord is not wanting anyone to perish** (2 Peter 3:9). He showed his willingness by providing **my servant**. How great is his love! Nor was Jesus an innocent pawn in the scheme of things. **The will of the LORD will prosper in** *his* **hand. He** (himself) **poured out his soul unto death.** He entered wholeheartedly into obedience of the Heavenly Father—willingly! Marvel at the grace of the Lord Jesus Christ!

Here is the ultimate death of the righteous, the death of the one who was intrinsically righteous. It was the death of this righteous one that alone made it possible for any and all others to also die the death of the righteous. But only through him. **For Christ died for sins, once for all, the righteous for the unrighteous, to bring you to God** (1 Peter 3:18). Here is the answer to Balaam's prayer, **'Let me die the death of the righteous.'** May it be so for you!

DYING FOR HEAVEN...?

DYING FOR HEAVEN...?

DYING FOR HEAVEN…?

DYING FOR HEAVEN...?

DYING FOR HEAVEN…?

DYING FOR HEAVEN...?

DYING FOR HEAVEN…?

DYING FOR HEAVEN...?

DYING FOR HEAVEN…?

DYING FOR HEAVEN...?

DYING FOR HEAVEN...?